W9-DEX-755

To:
From:

Contributing writers: Gail Cohen, Lain Chroust Ehmann, Georgann Gouryeb-Freeman, Judy Hershner, Katherine Q. Lyons, Kathryne Lee Tirrell

Cover photos: Cynthia Fliege, Christopher Hiltz, Shutterstock.com

Back cover photo: Getty

Interior photos: Dreamstime, Fotolia, Getty, Media Bakery, Shutterstock.com

New Seasons is a registered trademark of Publications International, Ltd.

Copyright © 2015 Publications International, Ltd. All rights reserved.
This book may not be reproduced or quoted in whole or in part
by any means whatsoever without written permission from:

Louis Weber, CEO
Publications International, Ltd.
7373 North Cicero Avenue
Lincolnwood, Illinois 60712

Permission is never granted for commercial purposes.

ISBN: 978-1-4508-9932-1

Manufactured in China.

8 7 6 5 4 3 2 1

Grandma & Grandchild

A Love to Treasure

new seasons®

THE DEAREST cradle in the world is a grandmother's arms.

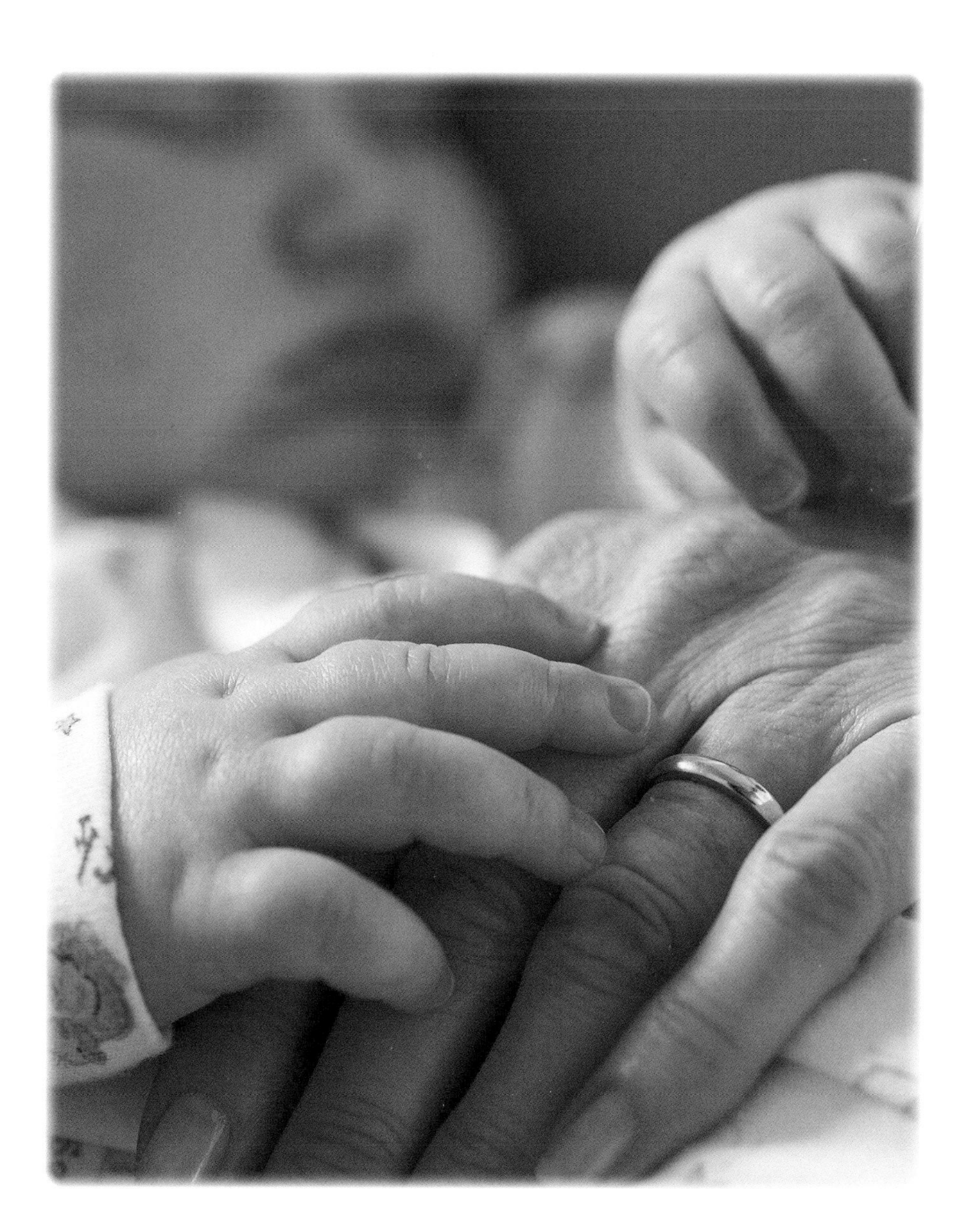

SOME PRECIOUS moments that slipped through the cracks of motherhood present themselves once more in the form of grandchildren.

GRANDMA'S HEART has countless rooms and many keys. Turn a lock and you'll discover an unlimited measure of tenderness, wisdom, hope, and forgiveness.

FOR A GRANDMOTHER, grandchildren are the best reminder that she will never outgrow her need to have fun.

A GRANDMOTHER'S love can be downloaded anywhere no matter how far away her grandchildren may go.

How do grandmas know exactly when
their grandchildren need them most?
Are they equipped with radar? Do they become clairvoyant?
Or is it simply having a sensitive heart,
open and waiting for the call?

AUTUMN LEAVES found on a walk
with grandma may be pressed in a book,
but the moment was pressed in her heart.

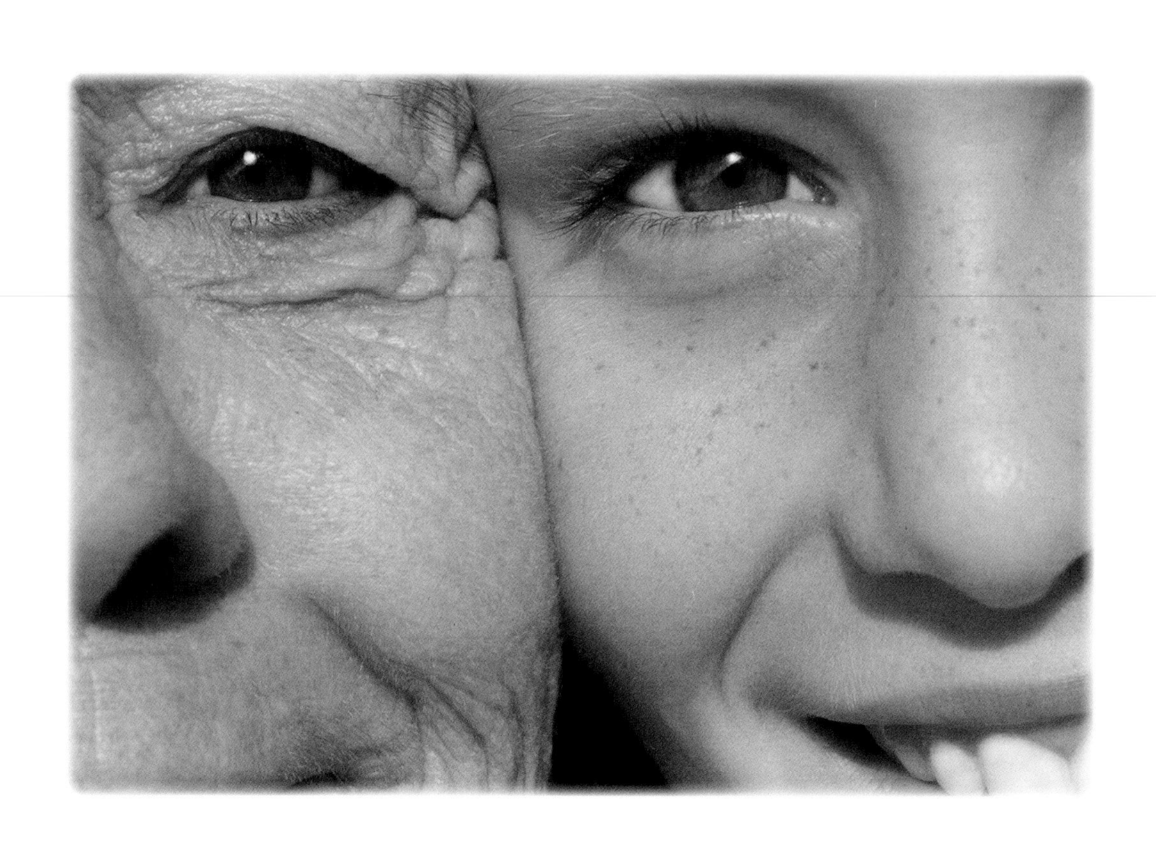

AGE MAY SHOW the difference in their skin,
but the love between family is timeless.

❂ ❂ ❂ ❂

FOR A GRANDMOTHER, every birthday with a grandchild is a present to herself.

GRANDMA'S TICKLES bring laughter
to her grandchildren that in turn tickle her heart.

WISE GRANDMOTHERS have the ability to guide and encourage several generations at the same time.

A TREASURED family heirloom is made from times spent with grandma, stitched together with love.

A GRANDMA will spoil you a little—it's true.
She'll bake you some cookies, some apple pie, too.
She'll tell you some stories; she'll sing lullabies;
she'll look at the world through
your wide-open eyes.

WHEN A WOMAN becomes a grandmother, she discovers a wonderful tonic against aging.

GRANDMAS ACT as though nothing else matters when their grandchildren come to them with a problem—whether it's a bruised knee or a broken heart.

A WOMAN'S patience and wisdom increase just in time to share with her grandchildren.

GRANDMOTHERS don't usually hurry as much as mothers, because they don't want life to go by any faster than it already does.

GRANDMOTHER is the keeper of family stories, little treasures, and an abundance of love.

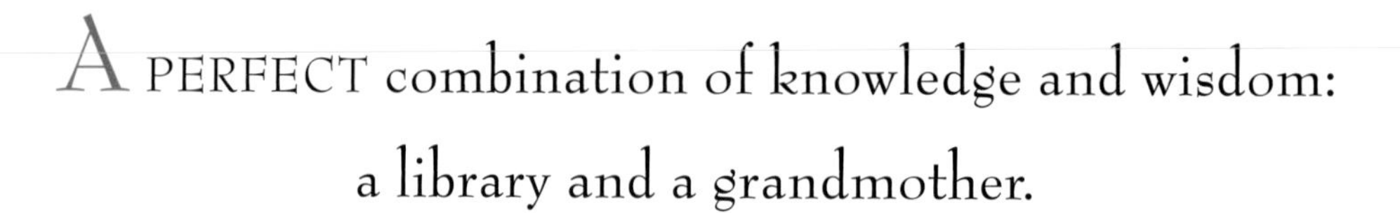

A PERFECT combination of knowledge and wisdom: a library and a grandmother.

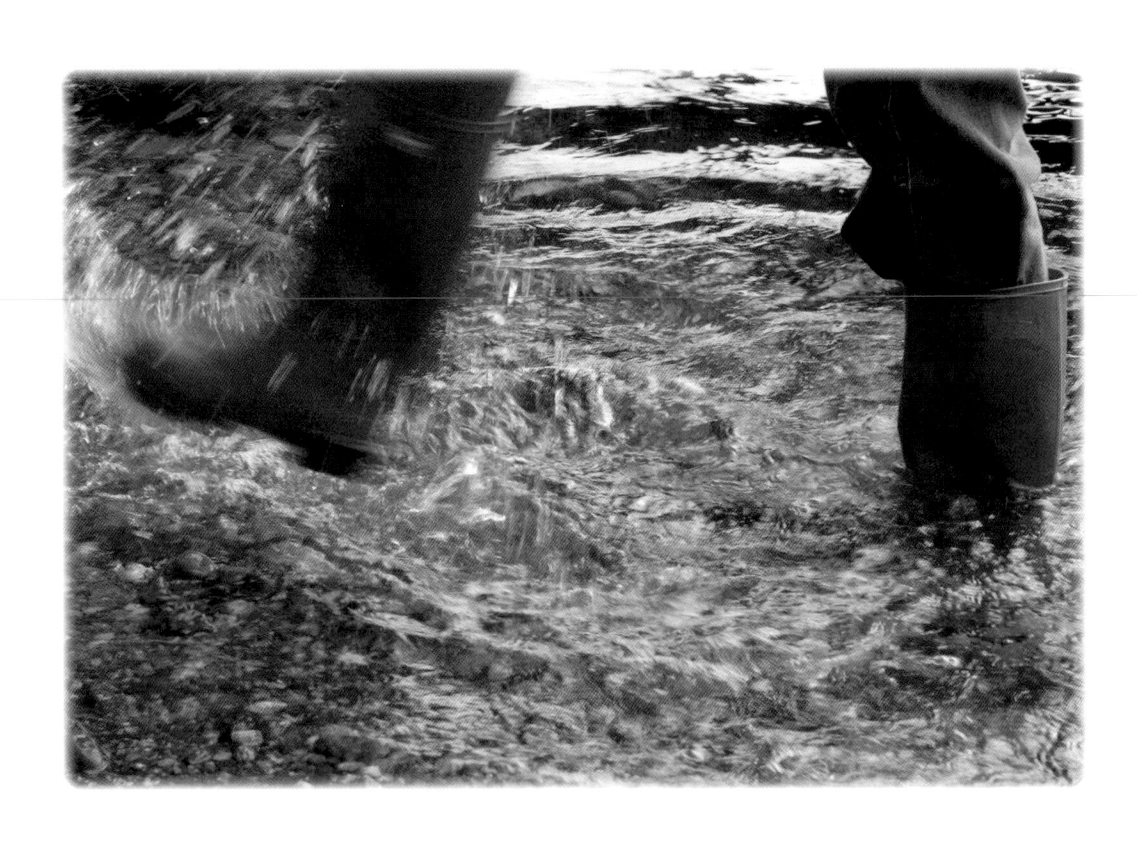

A GRANDMOTHER is never too old to splash in the puddles of life's rainy days.

A GRANDMOTHER who spends time with a child often imparts more faith than the words of a thousand sermons.

IT WAS THE AUTUMN of her life when the children left,
and spring when the grandchildren arrived.

IT IS AN IRONIC twist of fate that frees a woman after years of mothering, only to recapture her heart once again with grandmothering.

❁ ❁ ❁ ❁

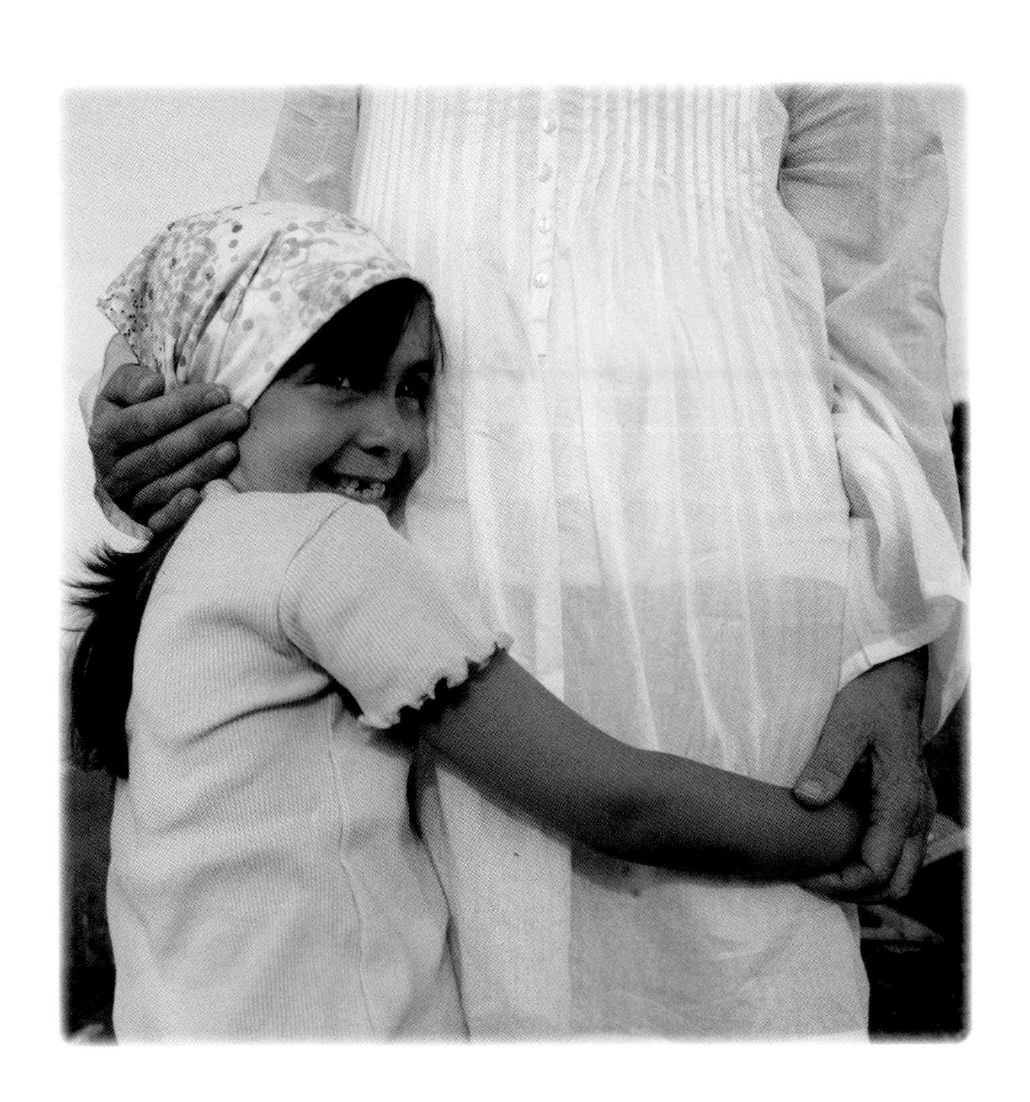

MEMORIES are made in grandma's kitchen
from wonderful aromas, laughter, love,
and many cups of tea.

IN HER GRANDCHILDREN'S faces she sees
her children's eyes, smiles, and love that has come full circle.

TIME SPENT with her grandchild guarantees a grandmother will feel younger merely by association.

GRANDMAS KNOW THAT it isn't important if
a house is clean, the dishes washed, and the laundry folded.
But they have the most unerring sense of what is
important—holding a small hand,
drying a freshly fallen tear, and taking time
to find their grandchild's favorite teddy bear.
Such is the wisdom of grandmas.

ALL TOO SOON a mother's stories are dismissed by her children until they provide her with a captive audience—her grandchildren.

THE ROAD FROM being a mother to a grandmother is paved with a few mistakes, a lot of experiences, and a heapful of love along the journey.

GRANDMOTHERS fill a special role in the lives of their grandchildren. They offer advice without agenda, playtime without distraction, and love without hesitation.

A WOMAN'S contract on mothering does not expire when her children grow up but rather gets an extension when she becomes a grandmother.

A WONDERFUL way to forget about the big things in life is to play with one of its little things: a grandchild.

A BRIDGE IS built between the future and
the past every time
a grandmother and grandchild hold hands.

THE BEST SEAT in the house is always on grandma's lap.

THE UPS AND DOWNS of mothering are just a ride on a swing for grandmothering.

GRANDCHILDREN may outgrow Grandma's lap,
but they never outgrow her love.